A POETRY

GW01451539

**ARIFICIALLY GENERATED POEMS
WRITTEN BY THE LATEST IN AI TECHNOLOGY**

http://amazon.com/author/stinger

STINGER PUBLISHING
STINGERPUBLISHING.COM
© COPYRIGHT 2023

As we stand on the cusp of a technological revolution, it is clear that Artificial Intelligence (AI) is changing the way we think about and interact with the world around us. In the realm of literature, AI has the potential to reshape the way we create and experience poetry. This book explores the cutting edge of AI-generated poetry, offering a glimpse into a new frontier of creative expression.

As you delve into the pages of this book, you will discover a wealth of poems crafted by algorithms and language models, each with its own unique voice and perspective. From hauntingly beautiful verse to absurdist experiments, the poems within will challenge your understanding of what is possible in the realm of AI-generated poetry.

At its heart, this book is a testament to the boundless potential of technology to augment human creativity. It is a celebration of the power of language to convey emotion and meaning, and a call to arms for poets, coders, and artists alike to continue pushing the boundaries of what is possible in this exciting new field.

So come, explore the wonders of AI-generated poetry with an open mind and a curious heart. I have no doubt that the poems within will leave a lasting impression on you, and spark a newfound appreciation for the power of technology to inspire and elevate the human spirit.

DISCLAIMER: The poems featured in this collection are the product of state-of-the-art AI technology, presented in their raw, unaltered form. While repetition in words and themes may occur, and grammatical refinement is still necessary, the reader is invited to draw their own conclusions about the tone and emotion conveyed.

INCLUDING THE FOLLOWING TYPES OF POEMS:

Sonnet - a 14-line poem written in iambic pentameter, with a specific rhyme scheme.

Haiku - a three-line poem with a 5-7-5 syllable count, often focused on nature.

Villanelle - a 19-line poem with a specific rhyme scheme and repeated lines.

Free verse - a poem with no specific rhyme or meter.

Ode - a poem that celebrates or praises a person, place, or thing.

Acrostic - a poem where the first letter of each line spells out a word or phrase.

Limerick - a humorous five-line poem with a specific rhyme scheme.

"Broken Sea Shells"

Broken Sea Shells on the shore,
Once a home, now forever more,
Fragile and shattered by the tide,
A story of beauty now denied.

A life once lived within their walls,
A place of safety, peace, and halls,
A home to creatures small and light,
But now they're just a memory in sight.

The waves they crash, the winds they blow,
Reducing shells to fragments below,
And yet, they hold a special grace,
A work of art in nature's space.

Though broken, they still glimmer bright,
With colors that dance in the light,
And though their homes are gone, they stand,
A symbol of beauty in the sand.

So let us cherish every piece,
Of these shells washed up on the beach,
For in their brokenness, they show,
The power of nature's ebb and flow.

Haiku: Mountains

Towering above us
Majestic peaks touch the sky
Silent guardians watch

"The Burden of Doubt"

The weight of doubt, it drags me down
A constant battle, I cannot drown
The voices in my head, they never cease
Whispering doubts, it's all a tease

But I must remember, I am strong
And I will carry on, no matter how long
For doubt is just a shadow, that fades with the light
And I am the master, of my own life

So I'll rise above, the doubts and the fear
And I'll face my challenges, with courage and cheer
For I am the one, who writes my own story
And I'll make it a journey, filled with glory.

Haiku: Waterfalls

Misty veil cascades
Rushing water crashes down
Nature's symphony

Haiku: Starry skies

Midnight's velvet cloak
Dotted with twinkling diamonds
Dreams take flight and soar

"Butterfly Effect"

The flutter of a wing, a small butterfly,
Can change the course of time, and the sky,
For every action, has a consequence nigh,
And the butterfly effect, is a lesson in why.

For every change, in the fabric of time,
A ripple is made, that will forever rhyme,
And the future is altered, by a single chime,
Leaving us with the mystery, of what we'll find.

So let us be mindful, in our travels through time,
For every step, is a choice that we make, a climb,
And the butterfly effect, is a constant reminder, that we'll find,
That every action has a consequence that will always shine.

Haiku: Beaches

Sandy toes sinking
Waves crashing on the shoreline
Ocean's lullaby

Haiku: Cherry blossoms

Delicate pink blooms
Fluttering in gentle breeze
Spring's fleeting beauty

"Acorn's Journey"

An acorn falls from the oak tree high,
Rolling and tumbling as it passes by.
It lands on the ground, with a soft, gentle thud,
The beginning of its journey, just begun.

The sun shines down, and the rain comes too,
The acorn starts to sprout, and it grows anew.
It reaches for the sky, its stem so strong,
Its leaves unfurl, and it sings a song.

It becomes a source of food and home,
For creatures great and small to roam.
Its branches stretch, its roots run deep,
A shelter for all, for all to keep.

And when it's old, and wise, and tall,
Its acorns will fall, and the cycle will call.
For the journey of an acorn never ends,
It's a story of growth, and life, which bends.

Haiku: Canyons

Carved by time's slow hand
Red rock walls rise up in awe
Nature's grandeur shines

"Calm of the Lake"

The sun is just rising, and the air is still cool,
As I make my way down, to the edge of the pool.
I cast my line out, and watch it slowly glide,
Into the calm of the lake, where the fish reside.

The sound of the water, and the birds in the trees,
Makes me forget, all of life's worries and pleas.
I breathe in the fresh air, and let out a sigh,
Feeling the peace, that fishing always supplies.

I wait for a bite, with patience and grace,
Feeling the pull, and the thrill of the chase.
As I reel it in, I can feel my heart race,
And I know, this is where I truly find my place.

Haiku: Yellow Flowers

Golden faces turn
Gazing at the summer sun
Bright petals unfurl

Haiku: Forests

Majestic green towers
Leaves rustle in gentle breeze
Peaceful sanctuary

"Adventure of the Sea"

The waves crash against the shore, and the wind whips my hair,
As I set sail, into the unknown, with nothing to compare.
The sea is vast, and the sky so blue,
An adventure awaits, and my heart feels anew.

I cast my line out, into the depths below,
Hoping to find, a treasure that I'll know.
The thrill of the catch, and the challenge of the sea,
Makes me feel alive, and so very free.

The sea is a mystery, and I'm just a part,
Of the journey it takes, from the start to the heart.
So I'll keep fishing, and following the tide,
And I'll always be searching, for the adventure of the sea inside.

Haiku: Autumn leaves

Rustling in the wind
Crimson, gold, and amber hues
Nature's canvas paint

Haiku: Rainbows

Seven colors bright
Arched across the stormy sky
Promise of sunshine

"All In the Journey"

The journey of life, is a long and winding road
Filled with ups and downs, that we must unload
With every step we take, and every choice we make
We shape our future, and forge our own fate

We encounter challenges that test our strength
And moments of joy, that lift us at great length
And through it all, we must find our way
With courage and hope, every step of the way

So let us cherish, each day that we're given
And make the most of it, with love and compassion
For life is a journey, full of mystery and surprise
And the memories we make, are our most precious prize.

Haiku: Snowy landscapes

Silent, still, and white
Frozen world in winter's grip
Quiet wonderland

Haiku: Lakes

Glassy surface calm
Reflections of sky and trees
Nature's mirror show

"Autumn's Harvest"

Golden leaves, rustling in the breeze,
The scent of apples, on the trees.
A day spent, among the orchard's pride,
With baskets filled, and joy inside.

The sun shines bright, and warms the earth,
As we wander, searching for the perfect girth.
Red and green, and yellow, too,
Hues of nature, in full view.

We pick and pluck, with care and love,
Each apple, a symbol, of the autumn's harvest above.
With crisp bites, and sweet aroma,
A taste of fall, like no aroma.

So let us cherish, this moment in time,
As we bask, in the autumn's prime.
With memories, to last a lifetime,
And a basket full, of the season's rhyme.

Haiku: Glaciers

Frozen rivers slow
Carving valleys through the land
Ice age monuments

"The Beach"

Sand between our toes,
The sun, shining bright.
Waves, gently rolling in,
Bringing peace, to sight.

The beach, a place of magic,
With memories, to treasure.
A place, where time stands still,
And all worries, beyond measure.

Sounds of seagulls, in the air,
The scent of salt, so sweet.
A place, where life is simple,
And our hearts, feel complete.

So let us walk, along the shore,
And bask, in the beach's roar.
For it is a place, of wonder,
And its magic, forever more.

Haiku: Deserts

Endless sea of sand
Sunburnt earth and rocky spires
Harsh and beautiful

"Beauty of the Forest"

The beauty of the forest, so serene and so wild,
A symphony of sounds, and a sight so beguiling.
With a canopy of green, and a carpet of brown,
And a peace that descends, and envelops the town.

The rustle of leaves, and the song of the birds,
The whisper of the wind, and the rustle of the ferns.
And the scent of the pines, and the sweet fragrance of flowers,
And the magic of the place, in those enchanted hours.

For the forest is a world, of its own design,
And it captures the heart, with its beauty so divine.
And it brings us closer, to the mystery of life,
And it opens our minds, to the wonders of sight.

Haiku: Seashells

Whispering secrets
Echoes of the ocean's song
Treasures from the shore

Haiku: Thunderstorms

Rumbling sky awakes
Lightning bolts across the clouds
Powerful display

"The Blossom's Colorful Bloom"

The flowers bloom, with a burst of color,
In a world so bright, that's full of wonder.
A rainbow of hues, in a vibrant display,
A show of beauty, that's here to stay.

The petals soft, in a gentle embrace,
A symbol of life, that's full of grace.
The fragrance sweet, in a heady scent,
A moment of peace, that's truly heaven sent.

So let the blossom, be your guide,
In a world of beauty, where you can find pride.
And feel its color, as it spreads its bloom,
In a show of life, that's truly a boon.

Haiku: Wildflowers

Colorful carpets
Sprinkling fields and meadows bright
Spring's delightful gift

Haiku: Hot springs

Steam rises and curls
Warm water soothes and relaxes
Nature's hot tubs

"The Blue Ocean"

The ocean, vast and blue,
A mystery waiting to be pursued,
With waves that crash and roar,
It whispers secrets that we've never heard before.

Its depths hold creatures unknown,
And its currents carry us home,
It's a place of peace and power,
And its beauty is a never-ending shower.

The ocean's rhythm never fails,
It lifts our spirits, calms our sails,
And reminds us of the world beyond,
A place where anything is possible and we all belong.

Haiku: Water lilies

Floating on the pond
Petals open to the sun
Peaceful beauty seen

Haiku: Sunsets

Golden sky ablaze
Colors bleed and blend to night
Serenity found

"Oceanic Symphony"

The ocean, a symphony,
A never-ending melody,
With notes of salt and sea,
It sings a song of mystery.

Its waves crash on the shore,
A symphony forever more,
And in its depths, a choir sings,
With harmonies that soothe our strings.

The ocean's rhythm never stops,
It's a beat that never drops,
And its rhythm calls us in,
A song of life, a symphony within.

The ocean, a mystery,
A symphony for you and me,
It whispers secrets in the breeze,
And sings a song of beauty and peace.

Haiku: Caves

Earth's hidden chambers
Mystery and adventure await
Secrets locked within

"Breaking Free from the Cube"

Breaking free from the cube, a moment so sweet,
A time to breathe, and to dance with your feet.
A time to explore, and to feel so alive,
A time to leave, the monotony behind.

The walls that confined, now far away,
And the chair so stiff, now a memory to sway.
And in this moment, you're free to be,
To laugh and to love, and to feel so alive.

For working in a cube, can often feel like a grind,
A place where the hours, can often be unkind.
But when the day is done, and you break free from the mold,
You'll find the world waiting, for your heart to unfold.

Haiku: Tidal pools

Hidden worlds revealed
Tide recedes, marine life shows
Window to the sea

Haiku: Cliffs

Rocky ledges high
Surf crashing on the rocks below
Nature's daring heights

"Cabin in the Mountains"

A cabin in the mountains, a place of peace,
Where the air is clear, and the world at ease,
With windows that look out to the hills,
And a fireplace that warms all our chills.

The sound of a stream, a song in the air,
A symphony that soothes, a lullaby to share,
The rustle of leaves, a whisper so mild,
A peacefulness that touches all that's wild.

The cabin is a refuge, a home away from home,
A place where one can be themselves, and never roam,
Where the mountain air is fresh, and the sky so clear,
And the sun sets over the peaks, a sight so dear.

The cabin in the mountains, a place of rest,
Where the days are filled with beauty, and nights with peace,
With a porch that overlooks the valley below,
And a view that takes your breath away, wherever you go.

The wood stove crackles, warming your soul,
As the wind howls outside, and the snow falls whole,
The smell of pine and cedar, a scent so true,
A reminder of the beauty that surrounds you.

The cabin is a sanctuary, a place of peace,
A place where the world is left behind, and you find release,
Where the mountains rise up, and the sky is wide,
And you feel at home, in this place, by your side.

"Choices"

In life, we make choices, every day,
Some small, some big, in our own way.
Each decision, shapes our fate,
And determines, our path and our mate.

We choose the words, we speak with care,
And the actions, we take without a scare.
We choose the friends, we keep close by,
And the dreams, we chase, up to the sky.

Our choices, define who we are,
And the life, we lead, near or far.
So let us choose, with wisdom and heart,
And make each choice, a brand new start.

Haiku: Fireflies

Glowing lanterns dance
Magical sparks in the night
Nature's fairy lights

Haiku: Icebergs

Glacier's castaway
Majestic and monumental
Journey through the sea

"Field of Grace"

A field of green, so vast and wide,
A carpet of grace, on which we stride.
The blades of grass, dance with the breeze,
A symphony of nature, that never cease.

The sun shines down, and warms the earth,
And the field of grass, it basks in its worth.
A place of peace, and calm, and rest,
A peaceful retreat, from life's hectic test.

It's a place to dream, and to play,
A place to forget, the worries of the day.
And when the night falls, and the stars come out,
The field of grass, shines with a gentle shout.

So when you need to escape, from the hustle and bustle,
Come to the field of grace, and let your soul rustle.

Haiku: Wildfires

Smoke fills the skyline
Flames consume the earth below
Nature's destructive force

"Firefighters"

Heroes in uniform, with courage in their hearts,
Ready to face danger, and make a brand new start,
With bravery and strength, they answer the call,
And rush to the fire, ready to save one and all.

With their fire trucks, and hoses at the ready,
They charge into the flames, with firefighting steady,
And with their training and skill, they battle the blaze,
And bring comfort and hope, in their own special way.

So let us take a moment, and thank our firefighters,
For their bravery and courage, that always inspires,
For they are heroes in uniform, who always stand tall,
And their selflessness and bravery, will never fall.

Haiku: Rainbow trout

Silvery scales flash
Fins cut through crystal clear stream
Catch and release joy

Haiku: Aurora borealis

Electric sky dance
Curtains of color twirl and wave
Nature's light show grand

"Grass's Story"

The grass, it grows, from the earth below,
A story untold, a mystery to know.
It reaches for the sky, its stem so strong,
A symbol of life, that lasts so long.

It's a home for creatures, both great and small,
A source of food, to help them stand tall.
And when the winds blow, and the rain comes down,
The grass bends low, and dances to the sound.

And when the winter comes, and the world turns cold,
The grass goes to sleep, and rests its hold.
But when the spring arrives, it awakes with cheer,
A new beginning, and a reason to be here.

So next time you walk, in a field of grass,
Remember this tale, and its story to amass.
A symbol of life, and growth, and hope,
The grass's story that will forever cope.

Haiku: Water spouts

Whirling vortex forms
Ocean's fury, windswept force
Nature's funnel cloud

"Gravel Road"

A journey on the gravel road, through the countryside so green,
With the wind in my hair, and the sun on my skin,
And the sound of the gravel, beneath the tires of my car,
As I travel down this road, so very far.

The fields stretch out, as far as the eye can see,
With the wheat and the corn, and the trees that sway in the
breeze,
And the birds singing, their sweet melodies so bright,
And the world feels alive, with such delight.

So I'll keep driving down, this gravel road so rough,
With the beauty of the world, that's more than enough,
And I'll savor each moment, as I travel down this path,
And make memories, that will surely last.

Haiku: Redwoods

Giant trees reach high
Majestic heights, peaceful groves
Nature's ancient keep

Haiku: Geysers

Steam from the earth's core
Water jets to the sky above
Nature's power awe

"Growing Old"

The beauty of growing old, a journey so grand,
A life so full of wisdom, a story so well planned.
With memories so sweet, and laughter so bold,
And a happiness so real, that shines so gold.

For growing old is a time, of growth and peace,
And a world so full of love, that will never cease.
And it's a time to reflect, on the journey we've been,
And a time to create, memories that will win.

So let's embrace the beauty, of growing old with grace,
And let's hold on tight, to the memories we'll trace.
For growing old is a time, of pure happiness,
And a world so real, that's full of bliss.

Haiku: Hummingbirds

Tiny wings a blur
Nature's flying jewels, they sip
Nectar with their beaks

Haiku: Tornadoes

Twister's whirling winds
Twisting through the land below
Nature's fury shows

"Chance to Start"

A new beginning, a chance to start,
With a heart full of hope, and a spirit so smart.
With dreams to chase, and goals to achieve,
And a life to live, with love and belief.

For life is a journey, full of twists and turns,
With ups and downs, and lessons to learn.
But with every step, and every breath we take,
We have the power, to shape our own fate.

So let's embrace the journey, with courage and grace,
And let's hold on tight, to the dreams that we chase.
For life is a gift, full of endless possibility,
And a new beginning, is a chance to live freely.

Haiku: Fields of lavender

Purple waves roll out
Scent of calm and peace surrounds
Nature's fragrant bliss

Haiku: Coral reefs

Rainbow colors glow
Tropical seas come to life
Nature's underwater show

"Inner Peace"

Finding inner peace, with a heart full of calm,
With a mind that's at ease, and a spirit so warm.
With moments of stillness, and peace that we find,
And a life to live, with love for all kind.

For life is a journey, with battles to fight,
With moments of peace, and days of delight.
But with every step, and every breath we take,
We have the power, to shape our own fate.

So let's find inner peace, with grace and with love,
And let's hold on tight, to the moments that we have.
For life is a gift, full of endless possibility,
And finding inner peace, is a chance to live happily.

Haiku: Hiking trails

Footsteps through the woods
Wilderness adventure calls
Nature's open book

Haiku: Thundering herds

Hooves pound on the plain
Buffalo roam wild and free
Nature's power reigns

"Majestic Shine"

The moon rises, in a world so calm,
In a gentle glow, that brings peace to all.
A ball of light, that shines so bright,
A symbol of mystery, that's full of might.

The sky turns silver, as the moon takes its place,
In a world so quiet, with a smile on its face.
The night begins, with a burst of peace,
A world of dreams, that never cease.

So let the moon, be your guide,
In a world of peace, where you can find pride.
And feel its light, as it shines so bright,
In a show of mystery, that's truly a sight.

Haiku: Sunbathed meadows

Summer's golden fields
Dappled light through swaying grass
Nature's simple joy yields

Haiku: Crashing waves

Ocean's song of power
Surf pounding on the shoreline
Nature's endless shower

"Salty Lips"

Salt on my lips, a reminder,
Of the sea and its endless tide,
A taste of the ocean, finer.

A kiss of the wind and spray,
As waves crash on the shore,
A memory to take away.

Of summer days and salty breeze,
And moments spent by the sea,
A time of joy and ease.

And as the salt lingers still,
A reminder of a simpler time,
Of peace and love that will always thrill.

So let the salt stay on my lips,
A memory of the sea,
A taste of a journey, a salty trip.

Haiku: Butterfly wings

Softly fluttering
Graceful dance through gardens bright
Nature's beauty brings

"Paradox of Time"

The past and the future, both in our reach,
With the present, a moment, that we cannot breach,
And the paradox of time, a riddle to teach,
As we journey through the ages, searching for peace.

For with every step, we take in this quest,
A change is made, in the timeline at best,
And the future is altered, a mystery to invest,
Leaving us with questions, that may forever be addressed.

So be careful my friend, in this journey so wild,
For time is a fragile thing, both gentle and mild,
And with every action, a change is compiled,
So tread lightly, for time is never mild.

Haiku: Rock formations

Carved by wind and rain
Stunning shapes in desert lands
Nature's art remains

Haiku: Cherry orchards

Pink blossoms everywhere
Scent of springtime fills the air
Nature's sweetest share

"Endless Horizon"

The ship sets sail, on the sea so blue,
With endless horizon, to guide us through.
The wind in our hair, the sun on our face,
We journey forth, to a brand new place.

The waves roll by, with a rhythmic beat,
A symphony of life, so serene and sweet.
The sea whispers secrets, of distant lands,
Of adventure and mystery, that's waiting to be manned.

So let the sea, be your guide,
In a world of wonder, where you can find pride.
And feel its breeze, as it takes you far,
In a journey of discovery, that's truly a star.

Haiku: Migrating birds

Vast flocks in the sky
Travelling across continents
Nature's wonders fly

Haiku: Volcanoes

Mountains born of fire
Smoking peaks and lava flows
Nature's fierce desire

"Touch of Rain"

The soothing touch of rain, a gentle caress,
A shower of blessings, that brings peace and rest.
A lullaby sung, by the winds that blow,
A melody that soothes, the soul below.

A cleansing of earth, a washing of the sky,
A gift from the heavens, that will never die.
A symphony of sound, as the raindrops fall,
A musical score, that's forever enthrall.

So let us embrace, the rain's gentle touch,
And be thankful, for its gift that's so much.
For it brings new life, and a world that's new,
The soothing touch of rain, a blessing that's true.

Haiku: Seashores

Shells scattered on the sand
Waves kissing the coastline's edge
Nature's gentle hand

Haiku: Thunderous water

Crashing on the rocks below
Majestic waterfalls
Nature's power show

"Good Neighbors"

The gift of good neighbors, a treasure so rare,
A source of comfort and a source of care.
With a smile and a wave, and a kind word to share,
And a shoulder to lean on, when life is unfair.

They bring joy to our lives, with their laughter and grace,
And they brighten our days, with their warm smile and face.
And they help us through life, with their love and their might,
And they lift us up, with their support and their sight.

So here's to the neighbors, who make life so sweet,
And who add to our days, a rhythm so beat.
For they are the ones, who make our lives bright,
And who bring us closer, with their gift of good light.

Haiku: Snow-capped peaks

Glittering in the sun
Pristine beauty of winter
Nature's white diamond

Haiku: Endless grasslands

Golden waves in the breeze
Majestic buffalo roam free
Nature's living seas

"Horse's Whisper"

The horse whispers, to the wind,
A secret so dear, that it can't be pinned.
A message of freedom, and of flight,
A story of life, bathed in light.

Their manes, they flow, with the wind's soft kiss,
A symbol of grace that they can't miss.
And when they run, they spread their wings,
A sight so beautiful, that it makes one sing.

The horse is a friend, to those who know,
A creature so gentle, that it can glow.
And when you're near, it will nuzzle your hand,
A sign of its love that it will always command.

So listen close, to the horse's whisper,
A secret so dear, that it will forever prosper.
A message of love, and grace, and life,
A story so beautiful, that it cuts like a knife.

Haiku: Canoe on the River

Paddling a canoe
Silent glide on the water
Nature's calm embrace

"The Sunset's Hues"

The day comes to an end, in a burst of flame,
As the sunsets, in a brilliant show of fame.
The sky ablaze, in hues of orange and red,
A canvas painted, that's nothing short of bed.

The world goes still, in a moment of peace,
As the sunset's beauty, cannot be beat.
The clouds take shape, in a surreal scene,
A masterpiece, that's truly serene.

So bask in the sunset's glow,
And feel its warmth, as it starts to grow.
For it's a moment, that's pure and true,
A reminder of beauty, that shines through.

Haiku: Coral

Life teeming under the sea
Rainbow fish and coral gardens
Nature's mysteries

Haiku: Dragonflies

Dragonflies in flight
Transparent wings glinting
Nature's aeronauts

"Miracle of Life"

The miracle of life, a story so grand,
A world so full of wonder, a feeling so planned.
With a heart that beats, and a soul that's new,
And a happiness so pure, that shines so bright and true.

For a baby is more, than just a tiny little one,
It's a journey so rich, a story that's just begun.
With laughter and tears, and joys that swirl,
And a symphony of life, that makes the world whirl.

So let's embrace the miracle, of life with open arms,
And let's hold on tight, to the memories that warm.
For a baby is a gift, from the heavens above,
And a miracle that's real, that we'll always love.

Haiku: Moonlit nights

Silver light bathes the land
Whispers in the night
Nature's peaceful grand

Haiku: Ancient ruins

Rubble and moss-covered stones
Nature's taking over
Her artfully overthrown

"Revenge"

The taste of revenge, so sweet and so sour,
With the desire for justice, in every moment of power,
And the satisfaction that comes, with every victory,
And the joy that we feel, with every enemy.

The urge for revenge, can be hard to ignore,
With the pain of injustice, and the wounds of war,
And the fire that burns, in the heart and the soul,
And the thirst for retribution, that never grows old.

So I'll seek revenge, with each step that I take,
Finding satisfaction, in each victory that I make,
Savoring the taste, of the sweet revenge,
And I'll revel in the power, at my victory's end.

Haiku: Forest creatures

Whispering through the trees
Rustling leaves and flitting wings
Nature's symphonies

Haiku: Fields of wheat

Rustling wheat fields
Golden fields of rolling grain
Nature's bounty yields

"Pain of Loss"

The pain of loss, a feeling so real,
A heart so broken, a wound that won't heal.
With tears that flow, and memories that last,
And a love that endures, from the present to the past.

For a loved one is more, than just a face we knew,
It's a part of us, a story that's always true.
With laughter and tears, and joys that swirl,
And a symphony of life, that makes the world whirl.

So let's embrace the pain, of loss with grace and peace,
And let's hold on tight, to the memories that will never cease.
For a loved one is a gift, from the heavens above,
And a love that endures, that we'll always hold with love.

Haiku: Sand dunes

Desert seas of sand
Wind sculpting forms in the dunes
Nature's artistry grand

Haiku: Spring rain showers

Pattering on the roof
Renewal and growth abound
Nature's sweet respite proof

"Slumbering Mind"

A mind that's tired, a body that's worn,
Sleep comes calling, a peaceful adorn.
The day is done, and dreams await,
A lullaby sung, by the night's soft grate.

The worries of life, slowly fade away,
As slumber takes hold, night and day.
In dreams, we soar, with ease and delight,
Till morning's dawn, brings a new sight.

So close your eyes, and let sleep take hold,
For a mind at peace, is worth more than gold.
Tomorrow's joys, await to unfold,
A slumbering mind is a story untold.

Haiku: Abandoned lighthouses

Stark and beautiful stands
Nature claiming her territory
Her artful, slow hands

Haiku: Desert landscapes

Spectacular sunsets glow
Colors of red, orange, and gold
Nature's canvas show

"Inevitable Change"

Embracing change, with open arms and a heart so bold,
With a spirit so free, and a story to be told.
With new adventures, and journeys to take,
And a life to live, with courage and faith.

For life is a journey, with roads that we choose,
With paths that we take and destinations, we lose.
But with every step, and every breath we take,
We have the power, to shape our own fate.

So let's embrace the change, with grace and with glee,
And let's hold on tight, to the dreams that we see.
For life is a gift, full of endless possibility,
And embracing change, is a chance to live freely.

Haiku: Harvest

Autumn harvest
Bounty gathered in the fields
Nature's feast for all

Haiku: Rolling hills

Sweeping fields of green
Rising and falling with the wind
Nature's tranquil scene

"Embrace of Sleep"

The gentle embrace of sleep, a comfort untold,
A lullaby sung, by the night's soft hold.
A place where worries, just fade away,
And where dreams take flight, night and day.

A world where anything is possible,
And where the mind can soar, so incredible.
Where the impossible, becomes the norm,
And where the heart can heal, from life's storm.

So let yourself be taken, by the gentle sway,
Of the night's embrace, and sleep's sweet sway.
For when you wake, you'll feel refreshed and new,
With the energy to face, what the day will do.

Haiku: Crystalline ice caves

Glimmering and frigid halls
Frozen in their beauty
Nature's glass-like walls

Haiku: Bubbling hot mud pools

Geothermal nature's show
Steam and mud from the earth
Nature's unique glow

"The Desert's Mirage"

The sand stretches out, in a world so vast,
In the desert's heat, where life moves fast.
A mirage of water, a trick of the light,
A glimpse of a dream, that's just out of sight.

The cactus stands tall, in a world so dry,
A symbol of life, that refuses to die.
The sun beats down, with a relentless force,
But the desert's beauty, is something of course.

So let the desert, be your guide,
In a world of heat, where you can find pride.
And feel its power, as it spreads out wide,
In a land of wonder, that's full of life.

Haiku: Sheep herding

Flocks of sheep
Woolly white clouds grazing
Nature's pastoral scene

Haiku: Ocean waves

Rolling ocean waves
Endlessly lapping the shore
Nature's soothing sound

"Time Waits for No One"

The sun rises high, in the morning sky,
And I'm still in bed, with a sigh and a cry,
For I know that time, waits for no one,
And I've lost another chance, to have a little fun.

The world moves on, without a second thought,
And I'm left behind, in a state that's wrought,
With regret and sorrow, for the time that I've sought,
And the opportunities, that I've let slip and got caught.

But still I stand, with my head held high,
For I know that time, can never die,
And I'll catch up soon, with a determined eye,
For I will not be late, and I will not say goodbye.

Haiku: Eagle's might

A soaring eagle
Riding the currents up high
Nature's majestic grace

Haiku: Open sky

The vast open sky
Endless and infinite blue
Nature's boundless view.

"The Waterfall's Voice"

The voice of the waterfall, a roar so grand,
A symphony so rich, a music so planned.
With water that falls, and mist that ascends,
And a beauty so vast, that never bends.

For waterfalls are the gifts, of nature so strong,
And they bring us the peace, of a life that's so long.
And they offer a show, of a power so true,
And they bring us the joy, of a world that's so blue.

So let's listen to the voice, of the waterfall so bright,
And let's cherish the gift, of its beauty so right.
For waterfalls are the treasures, of our world so rare,
And they bring us the peace, of a love that's so fair.

Haiku: Autumnal colors

Vibrant leaves falling down
Crimson, gold, and amber hues
Nature's changing gown

Haiku: Sandy deserts

Endless sea of dunes
Heat shimmering in the air
Nature's arid blooms

"Journey Homeward"

The road home, a journey I know well,
With the twists and the turns, and the memories I hold,
And the sound of the gravel, beneath my feet,
As I make my way, down the road so sweet.

The fields and the trees, a familiar sight,
And the smell of the earth, so fresh and light,
And the sky so blue, and the sun so bright,
And the world feels at peace, so very right.

So I'll keep walking down, this gravel road so dear,
With the memories I've made, and the ones still to clear,
And I'll savor each step, as I make my way back home,
And know that I'm blessed, to be here, all alone.

Haiku: Arctic tundra

Frozen wasteland vast and white
Wildlife roams in peace
Nature's unspoiled sight

Haiku: Fields of tulips

Rows of colors bright and bold
Spring's colorful show
Nature's beauty unfold

"The Vows of Love"

We stand before you, on this special day
With hearts full of love, in every way
To pledge our devotion, and our true love
In the vows of love, that we make above

With every kiss, and every embrace
Our hearts are filled, with a warm and loving grace
And as we stand here, hand in hand
We make our vows, to always stand

Together we'll face, the joys and the pain
And with each other, we'll never be in vain
For the vows of love, are sacred and true
And in our hearts, our love will always be new.

Haiku: Cherry tomatoes

Glossy spheres so bright
Plump and juicy to the taste
Nature's sweet delight

Haiku: Rustic barns

Weathered and aged with time
Surrounded by nature's growth
A charming sight sublime

"Journey through Dreams"

A journey through dreams, an adventure untold,
A world without bounds, with stories to unfold.
A place where the impossible, becomes the norm,
And where your mind's desires, take their form.

A land of magic, where the impossible takes flight,
Where the darkness of night, becomes the day's light.
A kingdom of wonder, where anything can be,
And the worries of life, just a distant memory.

So close your eyes, and let the journey begin,
Through the landscapes of dreams, with magic within.
Till morning comes, and you wake up anew,
With memories of wonders, forever in view.

Haiku: The Milky Way

A spiral in the night sky
Stars and planets shine bright
Nature's celestial high

Haiku: Ocean sunsets

Colors blazing on the waves
Peaceful and serene
Nature's quiet saves

"The Forest's Whisper"

The trees reach high, to the sky so blue,
In the forest deep, where the wind comes through.
A whisper of leaves, a rustle of breeze,
A symphony, of nature's own keys.

The forest floor, is a carpet of green,
A peaceful haven, where life is serene.
The animals roam, in a world of peace,
With the forest's whisper, a constant release.

So let the forest, be your guide,
In a world of peace, where you can hide.
And feel its calm, as it surrounds,
In a place of solace, where peace abounds.

Haiku: Camping under the stars

Sleeping In the great outdoors
Nature's cradle embrace
Dreams are nature's chores

Haiku: Desert oasis

Palm trees and a cool blue pool
Mirage in the sand
Nature's desert jewel

"The Sun's Radiant Glow"

The sun rises, in a world so bright,
In a burst of fire, that's full of light.
A ball of warmth, that brings life to all,
A source of energy, that stands so tall.

The sky turns orange, as the sun takes its place,
In a world so alive, with a smile on its face.
The day begins, with a burst of hope,
A new chance at life, with no end in sight.

So let the sun, be your guide,
In a world of hope, where you can find pride.
And feel its warmth, as it shines so bright,
In a show of life, that's truly a sight.

Haiku: Cloud formations

Cotton balls on the blue sky
Floating, shaping, drifting
Nature's dynamic high

Haiku: Fjords of Norway

Carved by ancient glaciers
Rising out of the sea
Nature's fjord explorer

"Time for Rest"

A time for rest, and a time for play,
Time to escape, from the chores of the day.
A time to forget, the worries of life,
And to bask in the sun, with a heart full of life.

A time to explore, new sights and new sounds,
To let your mind wander, and to unbound.
And when the day is done, to lay down with ease,
And watch the stars come out, as the world starts to freeze.

Vacation is a gift, a time to be free,
A chance to create, memories that will last eternally.
So don't let it slip, embrace each moment, each hour,
For vacation is a time, for a heart to flourish.

Haiku: Wandering rivers

Twisting and turning in the land
Flowing to the sea
Nature's guiding hand

Haiku: Wild horses

Running free on the plains
Manes and tails streaming
Nature's freedom reins

"Joy of Eating Out"

The joy of eating out, a delight to be sure,
With a menu to choose from, and flavors to explore.
And a server to greet you, with a smile so warm,
And a table set for two, or a gathering of a swarm.

From the bread and the butter, to the soup and the salad,
And the entrée that arrives, and takes center stage.
And the dessert that's offered, a sweet finale,
And the coffee that's poured, to end the day.

And the sights and the sounds, of a busy restaurant,
And the conversations that flow, as the meal is spent.
For eating out is more, than just a feast,
It's a time to connect, and a time to release.

Haiku: Coral beaches

White sand and crystal-clear seas
Shells and coral abound
Nature's treasure keys

Haiku: Misty mornings

Foggy veils shroud the land
Mystery and beauty
Nature's eerie band

"Lessons of Time"

The lessons of time, are often hard to learn
And with each passing day, they slowly turn
But they shape us, into who we are
And guide us, through the ups and downs, near and far

We learn of love, and we learn of pain
We learn of loss, and we learn of gain
And with each lesson, we grow and we mature
And face life, with a little more confidence, that's for sure

So let us embrace, the lessons of time
And learn from our mistakes, and never mind
For each moment, teaches us something new
And shapes us into, the person we're meant to be too.

Haiku: Autumn apples

Red, green, and yellow fruits
Crisp and juicy to the bite
Nature's harvest roots

Haiku: Wild waterfalls

Tumbling down the rocky cliffs
Majestic and free
Nature's waterfall gifts

"Late Again"

Another day, another chance to be late,
Running through the streets, feeling the weight,
Of the minutes that tick and the time that I waste,
Hoping to make it, before it's too late.

People hurry past, without a care,
As I stumble along, with my hair in a snare,
Thinking of all the things that I could have done better,
If only I'd gotten up a little earlier.

But still I press on, with a smile on my face,
For even though I'm late, I'm in the race,
And I know that I'll make it, no matter the pace,
For I am strong, and I can keep up the chase.

Haiku: Butterflies

Butterflies flutter
Wings like stained glass windows
Nature's painted skies

Haiku: Rolling thunder

Booming across the land
Echoes of power
Nature's stormy brand

"The Hiker's Medley"

I lace up my boots,
And hit the trail with glee,
With the rhythm of my footsteps,
And the music of the trees.

With each step, I feel the beat,
Of my heart and the land,
And the rhythm takes me higher,
To a place that I understand.

The melody of the mountain,
The harmony of the stream,
And the symphony of nature,
Is the music of my dream?

So I hike and I wander,
And I sing as I go,
With the music of the wilderness,
And the peace that it bestows.

Haiku: Fields of lavender

Purple blooms in endless rows
Fragrant and serene
Nature's perfumed flows

"Lasting Love"

A love that lasts, a treasure so rare,
With the beauty of the heart, and the care,
And the happiness that fills my soul, with each day,
And the joy that comes, with the love that stays.

The moments we've shared, have been so bright,
With laughter and tears, and moments of light,
And our love has grown, with each passing year,
And the happiness, that we hold so dear.

So, I'll cherish this love, and hold it tight,
And bask in the happiness, that shines so bright,
And I'll thank the heavens, for this gift so rare,
And the love that lasts, a treasure so fair.

Limerick about a Thunderstorm

There once was a storm in the sky,
With thunder that made the earth shake and sigh.
It was dark and quite loud,
With a flashing light crowd,
A thunderstorm, rolling on by.

"The Ocean's Rhythm"

The waves crash against the shore,
With a rhythm that's constant and pure.
The ocean's heartbeat, a soothing sound,
A symphony, that's truly profound.

The sea stretches out, as far as the eye can see,
A world of mystery, that's waiting to be.
The tides ebb and flow, with a grace so grand,
A never-ending dance, that's truly at hand.

So let the ocean, be your guide,
In a world of peace, where you can find pride.
And feel its rhythm, as it surrounds,
In a place of solace, that's truly profound.

Limerick about a Caterpillar

There once was a creature that crept,
Through the grass and the leaves, it adept.
It was fuzzy and round,
With feet all around,
A caterpillar, in no hurry to be kept.

"Hues at Sunset"

The hues of the sunset, a show so divine,
A canvas so rich, a beauty so fine.
With colors that blend, and light, that descends,
And a peace so real, that never bends.

For sunsets are the gifts, of nature so rare,
And they bring us the joy, of a world that's so fair.
And they offer a feast, of hues so bright,
And they bring us the peace, of a love that shines light.

So let's watch the hues, of the sunset so grand,
And let's cherish the gift, of its beauty so planned.
For sunsets are the treasures, of our world so true,
And they bring us the peace, of a love that shines through.

Limerick about a Firefly

There once was a bug with a light,
That shone in the dark of the night.
It was small, but quite bright,
And a magical sight,
A firefly, so enchanting and bright.

"Dirty Snowflakes"

Dirty snowflakes, fallen from the sky,
Once pure and white, now sullied and stained,
No longer a sight to fill the eye,
A symbol of man's environmental disdain.

From city streets to rural roads,
They've picked up grime, smog and soot,
A bleak reflection of our daily abodes,
And the toll our actions have put.

They're not the only ones affected,
Our air, water, and earth are too,
And unless we change, we'll be dejected,
By the world that we've let fall through.

So let's take action, and clean our skies,
And protect the beauty that surrounds us all,
And ensure that future snowflakes will arise,
Untainted and pure, a winter's snowfall.

Limerick about a Snail

There once was a creature so slow,
With a shell on its back, to and fro.
It would slide on the ground,
Without making a sound,
A snail, in no hurry to go.

"Loneliness"

The echo of loneliness, resounds within my heart,
A haunting melody, that won't depart,
It whispers secrets, of a life so incomplete,
And leaves me feeling, like I'm missing a beat.

The emptiness surrounds me, like a shroud,
And I'm lost in the shadows, of my own crowd,
And in the stillness of the night, I feel so alone,
With nothing but the echo, of my own moans.

But I know that I am not, truly alone,
For there is love and light, that I have known,
And I will hold on tight, to the memories that I hold,
And find comfort in the moments, that I'm not alone.

Acrostic poem for "WATERFALL"

Water cascades, down it flows,
A sight that calms, a sight that glows.
Thunderous and white, full of force,
Endless power, wild and hoarse.
Roaring through the rocks and stone,
Falling freely, all alone.
Awestruck, we watch and wait,
Listening to its serenade.
Luminous, a sight to see,
Lingering in memory.

"Life"

The miracle of life, is a wondrous thing
With each breath we take, our spirits take wing
It's the journey we make, from the day that we're born
To the day we leave, this world to mourn

We share the moments, with the people we love
And the memories we make, that we hold dear above
It's the laughter and tears, that make life complete
And the love that endures, through each heart beat

So let us cherish, the miracle of life
And make the most of it, without any strife
For it is a gift, that we must never waste
And the only thing, that we take with us, when we leave this place.

Acrostic poem for "CATERPILLAR"

Crawling slowly, inch by inch,
A caterpillar, in a pinch.
Transforming in a chrysalis,
Emerging with wings, pure bliss.
Roly-poly, soft and round,
Persevering on the ground,
Illuminated by the sun,
Living life, a slow-motion run.
Little friend, so hard at work,
Alive and vibrant, never a quirk,
Reborn anew, a butterfly,
Fluttering in the summer sky.

"Slice of Heaven"

A food for the soul, so warm and so bright,
A treat for my spirit, a love so true and right.
With melted cheese, and toppings so grand,
A bite of this pie, I'll take by hand.

For pizza is more, than just bread and sauce,
It's a story so rich, a world so porous.
With flavors that lift, and spices that swirl,
A symphony of love, that make the world twirl.

So let's raise a slice, to this food so pure,
And let's enjoy each bite, with joy that will endure.
For pizza is a gift, from the gods above,
And a food for the soul, that we'll always love.

Acrostic poem for "THUNDER"

Thunder rolls across the sky,
Heralding a storm gone by.
Undulating through the air,
Nature's music, loud and rare.
Deep and rumbling, strong and true,
Echoes through the world anew.
Ringing out across the land,
Thunder's power, wild and grand.

"Lonely Road"

The lonely road, stretches out before me,
With emptiness and silence, as far as the eye can see,
And as I walk this path, I feel so all alone,
With nothing but my thoughts, as my only known.

The wind whispers secrets, that I cannot comprehend,
And the stars shine bright, like diamonds, in the sky above,
And though I know that I am not alone, in this world so wide,
I can't shake the feeling that I'm just passing by.

So I'll keep walking down, this lonely road I've chosen,
With hope and faith, that one day, I'll find my true home,
And the loneliness will fade, and the emptiness will cease,
And I'll find peace and love, and be forever at peace.

Acrostic poem for "BUTTERCUP"

Beneath the sun, a flower bright,
Unfolds its petals with delight.
The buttercup, a thing of grace,
Twinkles gold upon its face.
Each bloom, a tiny cup of cheer,
Reflects the light so crystal clear.
Coming to life in the spring,
Up from the earth, a hopeful thing.
Playful, pretty, full of glee,
A gift of nature, bright and free.

"The Journey Home"

The trail is winding down,
And the journey's almost done,
With the memories and the moments,
That will last for years to come.

The sun sets on the mountain,
And the shadows grow long,
And I know that I will always,
Remember where I belong.

So I walk with a lighter heart,
And a smile upon my face,
With the peace that only nature,
Can bring to this place.

And as I reach the end,
I know that I am home,
With the journey of a lifetime,
And the memories I've known.

Limerick about a Hummingbird

There once was a bird with great speed,
Whose wings were so quick, they'd exceed.
It was small as a bee,
But as fast as could be,
A hummingbird, with grace, it would feed.

"The Union of Two"

We come together, in the union of two
With hearts full of love, and dreams so true
To join our lives, and become one
In the union of two, under the sun

With every step, and every breath
We'll build a life, filled with love and rest
And as we stand here, side by side
We'll face the world, with love as our guide

So let us vow, to cherish each day
And hold each other, in every single way
For in the union of two, we're never alone
And with each other, our love will forever grow.

Acrostic poem for "DAFFODIL"

Dancing in the springtime breeze,
A flower that fills us with ease.
Flashing yellow, so bright and bold,
Fragrant, sweet, and full of gold.
On the fields and gardens they stand,
Daffodils, a sight so grand,
In a world reborn and freshly tanned,
Laughing with joy, oh how they expand!

"The Summer Rain"

The sun shines bright, on a summer's day,
But a rainstorm comes, in a sudden way.
The drops fall down, in a gentle mist,
A cooling touch, that's pure bliss.

The world comes alive, in a symphony,
Of sound and color, so vibrant and free.
The flowers bloom, in a burst of hue,
With the rain's touch, they come anew.

So let the rain, wash away your cares,
And dance in the downpour, without a care.
For the rain is a gift, that brings life,
And a moment of peace, in a hectic life.

Acrostic poem for "RAINBOW"

Red, orange, yellow, green, and blue,
A spectrum of colors that's brand new.
In the sky after the rain,
Nature's art is on full display,
Beauty and wonder that will never wane,
Oh, how we love the rainbow's bright array!
When the storm is gone and the sun breaks through.

"Love Conquers All"

Love is a force, that conquers all,
A feeling, that stands tall.
Against the winds, and raging seas,
With a power, that sets us free.

Love is a light, that shines so bright,
In the darkness, it brings us sight.
It lifts us up, and gives us hope,
And helps us cope, with life's slippery slope.

Love is a bond, that cannot break,
A connection that will never shake.
It brings us joy, and peace of mind,
And makes us whole, of body and of kind.

So let us love, with all our might,
And hold on tight, with all our might.
For love is life, and life is love,
A gift, sent from heaven above.

Acrostic poem for an "EAGLES"

Eagles fly, high above,
A symbol of strength and love.
Graceful in their flight,
Looking down on us with might.
Eyes sharp and keen,
Soaring through the sky, serene.

"Lucky Penny"

The lucky find, a penny from the sky,
With the shine of hope, and the gleam of light,
And the smile that comes, with this small surprise,
And the happiness, that's hard to disguise.

The roads I've walked, have been long and hard,
With the trials of life, and the heavy heart,
And the lucky find, has brought a ray of hope,
And the happiness, that I'll always know.

So, I'll hold this penny, and hold it tight,
And bask in the happiness, that shines so bright,
And I'll thank the heavens, for this lucky find,
And the smile that comes, with the love in mind.

Acrostic poem for "OTTER"

Oh, how the otter loves to play,
Twisting, turning, swimming all day.
They slide on rocks and splash in the sea,
Eager to show off their agility and glee.
Running along the riverside,

"One Mind's Journey"

A journey of the mind, to a place so bright,
A place of peace, where worries take flight.
A place of sun, and sand, and sea,
Where you can be, who you want to be.

A place of laughter, and joy, and love,
A place of memories, from the heavens above.
And when the journey ends, and you return to life,
You'll carry with you, a world of light.

Vacation is a dream, that comes true,
A chance to escape, and to start anew.
So take it all in, each sight and each sound,
For vacation is a journey, that knows no bounds.

Ode to a Dandelion

Oh, dandelion, humble weed,
You are the bravest one indeed.
You sprout up from the ground below,
Despite the wind and rain and snow.

Your golden head, so full of light,
Is like a star that shines so bright.
And when the wind begins to blow,
You scatter seeds that soon will grow.

You bring us joy and endless cheer,
Your simple beauty draws us near.
So here's to you, dear dandelion,
The flower of the common man.

"Majestic Creatures"

With grace and beauty, they roam the land,
The horses of the fields, with a spirit so grand.
Their powerful bodies, move with such ease,
A sight to behold, with their manes that breeze.

Their eyes, so wise, hold knowledge deep,
A story untold, that they keep.
And when they run, their hooves pound the ground,
A thunderous rhythm, that knows no bound.

The horse is a symbol, of strength and might,
A creature of grace, that shines so bright.
From the rolling hills, to the prairies vast,
The horse is a treasure that will always last.

Acrostic poem for "SUNRISE"

Soaring high, the sun makes its ascent
Up from the horizon, its rays so bright
New light fills the world, and we're content
Rousing us from slumber, with its light so right
Reflecting on the sea, it's a sight so serene
Illuminating all the world, a morning's dream
Showing us the start of a brand new day
Enveloping us in light, in its warm ray

"Family Tradition"

Every year, as fall draws near,
We gather, with family and cheer.
To the orchard, we make our way,
For a tradition, that will never fade away.

We laugh and play, and pick with care,
With baskets filled, and hearts to spare.
The children run, with joy and glee,
And the elders, recall, with memories.

The apples, crisp and red, so bright,
A symbol, of love, and family's might.
We bring them home, and bake with glee,
Making pies, and sharing with family.

So let us cherish, this yearly quest,
With love and laughter, at its best.
For apple picking, is more than just a treat,
It's a bond that cannot be beat.

Acrostic poem for "CANYON"

Carved by the force of water, so strong
A natural wonder, that's been here long
Nature's grandeur, in every crevice and peak
Years of erosion, the canyon does speak
On the ground, we stand in awe
Navigating the depths, with a sense of awe

"Darkness"

The mystery of the moonlit night, with the stars so far away,
And the moon so full and bright, with a light that's here to stay,
And the world so still and silent, with only the sound of the night,
And the secrets that fill my mind, with such delight.

The wind carries whispers, of things I cannot see,
And the shadows dance, with a mystery,
And the beauty of the night, holds the key,
And I'm lost in the mystery, of this moonlit sea.

So I'll wander and wonder, and bask in the light,
And let the mystery fill me, with delight,
And I'll cherish this moment, for all of my life,
And know that the moonlit night, holds a secret that will never die.

Acrostic poem for "OASIS"

Over the dunes, a vision we see
A place of respite, an oasis, it be
Soothing green palms, with water so pure
Isolated from the desert's great lure
Serene and quiet, it's quite a sight

"Moonlit Romance"

The romance of the moonlit night, with the stars above aglow,
And the moon so full and bright, with a light that's soft and slow,
And the world so still and peaceful, with only the sound of the
night,
And the love that fills my heart, with such delight.

The breeze whispers sweet nothings, in my ear,
And the shadows dance, with a grace that's dear,
And the beauty of the night, holds me so near,
And I'm lost in the romance, of this moonlit year.

So I'll hold my love close, and bask in the light,
And let the romance fill me, with delight,
And I'll cherish this moment, for all of my life,
And know that the moonlit night, is a love that will always survive.

Acrostic poem for "FIREFLY"

Flying in the night, like a lightning bug
Illuminating the sky, with its soft hug
Radiating light, like a miniature sun
Enlightening us, with its lovely fun
Flitting in the air, like a silent song
Leaving us awed, all night long
Yielding its beauty, to which we belong

"Broken Down Car"

My rusty companion, a car that has seen,
Years of wear and tear and roads full of green.
A car that has taken, me everywhere,
And has never failed, to take me anywhere.

But now it's broken down, a sight to behold,
And it seems as though, its journey's grown old.
The engine it sputters, and the wheels they do creak,
And I'm left to ponder, what it is I seek.

But still I hold on, to this car that I love,
For it's a part of me, and it's come from above.
And I'll fix it up, and I'll make it brand new,
For it's my trusty companion and I won't abandon it true.

Acrostic poem for "THUNDER"

Thunderbolt, with its explosive sound
Heralding the storm, that's coming around
Under the sky, it crackles and rumbles
Nature's grandeur, in its power, humbles
Dancing in the air, with its electric flow
Erupting in the night, with its fiery glow
Raging through the clouds, it does show

"Long Proud Legacy"

The legacy of the Native Americans, that echoes through time,
With the rich culture, and the traditions so fine,
And the wisdom of the elders, that still lives on,
And the pride of the people, that shines so strong.

The beauty of their land, and the spirit of their kin,
With the love of their customs, and the music they spin,
And the reverence for nature, that they hold so dear,
And the strength of their spirit, that's so crystal clear.

So we honor their legacy, with every step we take,
And we cherish their culture, for the wisdom it brings,
And we pay homage to their courage, and their might,
And we keep their traditions, shining bright.

Acrostic poem for "HONEYCOMB"

Heavenly sweet, the honeycomb
On a summer's day, it's easy to roam
Nurtured by bees, it's a nature's delight
Emanating a fragrance, that's simply bright
Yellow and gold, the honey it holds
Creating a buzz, as the story unfolds
Oozing with sweetness, like no other
Making it a treasure, like a gift from mother
Beauty and bounty, in the honeycomb

"A New Dawn"

The sky ablaze with orange and pink,
As the sun rises with a gentle shrink.
A new day, a new dawn, a new start,
With endless possibilities that tug at our heart.

The world awakens, creatures stir,
A symphony of birds chirp and purr.
The cool air dances on our skin,
And the dew on the grass glistens like a grin.

A new dawn, a new chance, a new lease on life,
To chase our dreams, to live without strife.
So let's embrace this new day with grace,
And bask in the warmth of the morning's embrace.

Acrostic poem for "HURRICANE"

Howling winds, that rage and pound
Under the sky, it's a storm unbound
Rain that pelts, like bullets in flight
Radiating fear, with all its might
In the face of it, we cling and hold tight
Curving in the wind, with a powerful might
And in the eye of the storm, it's quite a sight
Nature's fury, it's a sight of fright
Enduring its power, with all our might

"Endless Possibilities"

The fabric of time, a mystery untold,
A journey through the ages, yet to unfold,
With endless possibilities, both young and old,
And secrets waiting, to be uncovered and hold.

Through portals and gates, to different lands,
With memories and moments, held in our hands,
The past, the present, and the future all blend,
In this journey, that time travel extends.

And who knows what lies, in the pages of time,
With wonders and mysteries, that will forever shine,
So let us embark, on this journey so fine,
And discover the secrets, that time travel can find.

Acrostic poem for "STARFISH"

Silent and serene, the starfish lies
The orange and pink, it's a sight to surmise
A creature of the sea, it's a natural prize
Radiating beauty, with its five-point guise
Fascinating and unique, in its own guise
In the waves, it's a delicate surprise
Swimming with ease, it's like it flies
How we adore the starfish, in all its size

"Lullaby of the Stream"

Oh gentle stream, with your soft and soothing sound
You glide and sparkle, as you make your rounds
Winding and flowing, through fields and through towns
Bringing life to all, with your gentle sounds

As you gurgle and murmur, so calm and so bright
You sing a sweet song, in the still of the night
And though the world may change, and the moon may take flight
Your melody lingers, with the stars shining bright

With every step, that I take by your side
Your rhythm and grace, I cannot help but abide
And as I listen, my heart is filled with pride
For the gift of your presence, that I cannot hide

So let me lay down, and close my weary eyes
With the lullaby of the stream, as my lullaby of the skies
And know that the world is alright, under your spell
For in your embrace, all my worries do dispel

So sleep my dear child, and dream of this place
Where the stream sings a song, of love, peace and grace
And when you wake, with a smile on your face
You'll know that this world is a beautiful place.

Acrostic poem for "FERN"

Fringed and delicate, the fern stands
Enveloping the ground, with its green bands
Radiating a calm, that's simply grand
Nurtured by nature, it's like a natural strand

"Parenthood"

The joy of parenthood, a feeling so rare,
A world so full of laughter, a story that's fair.
With hearts that beat, and souls that grow,
And a happiness so pure, that we can all know.

For a baby is more, than just a bundle of joy,
It's a journey so rich, a story that's never dull or void.
With laughter and tears, and joys that swirl,
And a symphony of life, that makes the world whirl.

So let's embrace the joy, of parenthood with care,
And let's hold on tight, to the memories that are so rare.
For a baby is a gift, from the gods above,
And a joy that's real, that we'll always love.

Acrostic poem for "SEASHELL"

Soothing and serene, the seashell lies
Enveloping the shore, with its sandy guise
A treasure of the sea, it's easy to surmise
Shaped like a cone, with a polished rise
Holding secrets, that's hidden from our eyes
Every color and pattern, it's quite a prize
Living in the sea, it's where it thrives
Loved by many, it's a seaside vibe

"The Morning Mist"

The dawn breaks, with a gentle kiss,
And the mist rises, like a lover's bliss.
A veil of mystery, a shroud so light,
A moment of peace, before the day's bright light.

The world awakes, in a silent hush,
As the mist clears, with a gentle rush.
And the sun rises, with a warm embrace,
A new day dawns, with its own grace.

So bask in the mist, as it slowly fades,
And feel its calm, as it gently serenades.
For it brings peace, and a new start,
And the hope of a day, filled with a loving heart.

Sonnet: Waterfall

A waterfall, majestic in its grace,
That tumbles down, with force and sheer delight,
It paints a picture, with water's lace,
And fills the air, with mist and rain in flight.

It carves its way, with power and a roar,
And etches out a path, with every drop,
It sings its song, and dances evermore,
A natural wonder, that never stops.

It paints the rocks, with colors that shine,
And forms a pool, that's crystal clear and deep,
A tranquil place, where nature's quite divine,
And all around, its beauty we can keep.

Oh waterfall, you're nature's grandest art,
A wonder that forever fills our heart.

"Peace"

The peace within, is where we find our calm
In the stillness of our hearts, and the quiet of our soul's palm
It's a place of refuge, from the storms of life
Where we find solace, and ease from the strife

It's the place where we go, when we need to heal
And find comfort, in the memories that we feel
And it's the place where we find, our inner peace
And the strength to carry on, in any crisis or siege

So let us cherish, the peace within our hearts
And find refuge, whenever life tears us apart
For it is the foundation, of our strength and our might
And the source of hope, in the darkest of night.

Limerick about a Wave

There once was a swell in the sea,
That crashed on the shore so wildly and free.
It was a force to be reckoned,
And with each swell beckoned,
A wave, so powerful, just wait and see.

Sonnet: Mountain path:

A mountain path, winding and wild,
With stones and roots that twist and wind,
A journey of ascent, that's quite beguiled,
And yet, we press on, and leave the grind.

Through canopies of green, it meanders and flows,
The trees embracing us, like an old friend,
And as we climb, the path ever grows,
And leads us to a place, where we can mend.

The air grows thin, as we climb ever high,
And the vista, it opens up to our view,
We pause and breathe, with a happy sigh,
And all around, nature's beauty does ensue.

The mountain path, a journey of the soul,
With every step, we find our spirit whole.

Limerick about a Sunflower

There once was a flower so tall,
With a face that would follow the fall.
It was bright as the sun,
And as big as a bun,
A sunflower, growing so grand and so tall.

"Journey through Life"

Life is a journey, with twists and turns,
Ups and downs, that we must learn.
To navigate, with grace and ease,
Embracing change, with the winds that breeze.

With each step, we grow and evolve,
Discovering ourselves, and what we involve.
In this grand adventure, filled with delight,
We must trust, and embrace the light.

For every storm, and every strife,
There is a lesson, to enrich our life.
And though the road may seem unclear,
We must have faith, and persevere.

For the journey, is the reward,
Filled with memories, to be cherished and adored.
So let us travel, with courage and glee,
Embracing life, and all it will be.

Acrostic poem for "GLACIER"

Glistening ice, that glimmers and shines
Leaving its mark, as it moves and reclines
A glacier, a marvel of nature so great
Carving the earth, with its weighty weight
In the midst of the arctic, it does stand
Enveloped in the mist, like a mystical band
Radiating a cold, that's beyond our command

"A Car I Once Knew"

The car that I knew, was once so strong,
With wheels that would roll, and an engine so long.
It would take me places, with a hum and a purr,
And I'd feel so free, with the wind in my hair.

But now it's broken down, and it's left me forlorn,
With a heart that aches, and a head that's worn.
For this car that I knew, has seen better days,
And I'm left to ponder, in so many ways.

But I'll fix it up, I'll bring it back to life,
And I'll drive it once more, without any strife.
For this car that I knew, is a part of me,
And I'll keep it running, for all eternity.

Limerick about Coffee

There once was a brew that we love,
A drink that we savor and shove,
It's coffee, the elixir,
With a flavor so rich and so pure,
A beverage we always approve.

"Finding Money"

The surprise of money, a gift from the sky,
With the shine of hope, and the gleam of light,
And the smile that comes, with this unexpected prize,
And the happiness, that's hard to disguise.

The roads I've walked, have been long and rough,
With the trials of life, and the heavy heart,
And the surprise of money, has brought a ray of hope,
And the happiness, that I'll always know.

So I'll hold this money, and hold it tight,
And bask in the happiness, that shines so bright,
And I'll thank the heavens, for this surprise so sweet,
And the love that's found, with the two feet.

Limerick about Road trips

On the road, we roam and we fly,
With the windows down, we see the sky,
Through winding turns and bends,
Our journey never ends,
Road trips, the adventure that we can't deny.

"Sound of Rain"

The sound of rain, so gentle and so true,
A lullaby sung, that brings peace to you.
A symphony of sound, as the raindrops fall,
A melody that soothes, the soul of all.

A pitter and patter, a tap and a thud,
The raindrops they fall, like a gentle caud.
A rhythm so soothing, a beat all its own,
A song that's forever, in the heart its known.

So let us listen, to the rain's gentle tune,
And be comforted, by the rhythm of the moon.
For it brings a calm, that's like no other sound,
The sound of rain that will always be found.

Limerick about a Ladybug

There once was a beetle so red,
With black spots on its back, it's been said.
It was small as could be,
But quite lovely to see,
A ladybug, on a leaf overhead.

"Man's Best Friend"

My faithful friend, a dog so true,
With eyes that sparkle, and a tail that wags too.
A companion through thick and thin,
And a love that has no end within.

With fur so soft, and a tongue so wet,
And a bark that's gentle, you'd never forget.
And when I'm feeling down, with a nuzzle and a kiss,
You lift me up, and my day you bless.

For you are more, than just a pet,
You are a friend that I won't forget.
And I'm so grateful, for the love that you bring,
My faithful friend, a treasure beyond anything.

Limerick about Gardening

In the garden, we dig and we sow,
With the sun on our backs, we watch it grow,
We plant our seeds and we tend to our beds,
With the flowers blooming, our heart is fed,
Gardening, the beauty that we show.

"To Overcome"

Overcoming adversity, with strength and with might,
With a spirit so fierce, and a heart full of light.
With courage to face, and battles to win,
And a life to live, with passion within.

For life is a challenge, with obstacles to overcome,
With trials and tests, and battles to be won.
But with every step, and every breath we take,
We have the power, to rise and to break.

So let's embrace the challenge, with grace and with might,
And let's hold on tight, to the dreams that we fight.
For life is a journey, full of endless possibility,
And overcoming adversity, is a chance to live freely.

Limerick about Dancing

With music in the air, we dance and we sway,
In perfect rhythm, our worries go away,
Our bodies move in harmony,
Our spirits lifted, so carefree,
Dancing, the joy that comes our way.

"The Pursuit of Happiness"

I chase the sun, across the sky
In search of happiness, that I cannot deny
I journey far, I journey wide
In search of the things, which make me thrive

For happiness is a treasure, that we all desire
A state of mind, a warm inner fire
It's the simple things that make us smile
The laughter, the love, the memories all the while

So I'll keep searching, with a heart so light
And I'll find my way, to the shining light
For happiness is within, and it's ours to find
And it's a journey, that we'll never leave behind.

Limerick about Star gazing

In the night, we look up and we see,
A universe so vast and so free,
With stars twinkling up above,
We're lost in wonder and love,
Star gazing, the beauty that we agree.

"The Starry Night"

The sky ablaze, with twinkling lights,
A canvas painted, with stars so bright.
Each one a gem, in a sea of black,
A breathtaking sight, that won't come back.

The moon shines down, with a silver beam,
A gentle guide, in this starry dream.
The night so still, so peaceful, so serene,
With stars that dance, in a celestial scene.

So gaze up high, and let your heart soar,
With each star a wish, you'll want more.
And in this night, so rich and vast,
Find peace and joy that will always last.

Limerick about the Beach

On the sand, we lie and we bask,
With the sun on our skin, it's a grand task,
The waves rolling in and out,
We're lost in thought, without a doubt,
Beach, the haven where we relax.

"Passed"

Remembering a life lived, a story so grand,
With laughter and tears, a journey so planned.
With hearts that beat, and souls that soar,
And a love that endures, forever more.

For a loved one is more, than just a memory,
It's a part of us, a legacy.
With joys that swirl, and love, that's true,
And a happiness so pure, that shines through and through.

So let's embrace the memories, of a life lived with care,
And let's hold on tight, to the love that's always there.
For a loved one is a gift, from the gods above,
And a life remembered, that we'll always hold with love.

Limerick about Cooking

In the kitchen, we chop and we cook,
With the flavors blending, it's like a book,
We savor every bite and taste,
With every dish, our palate's chased,
Cooking, the magic we undertook.

"Sea of Hues"

A sea of colors, so bold and so bright,
As the leaves of fall, take to flight.
An ocean of hues, so rich and so grand,
As the autumn winds, blow through the land.

The yellow and the orange, so warm and so bright,
The red and the gold, so bold in their sight.
All blending together, in a tapestry so bold,
A sight to behold, that never grows old.

So let us cherish, this view so serene,
And bask in the beauty, of fall leaves so green.
For soon they will fade, and the winter winds blow,
Leaving behind, a sea of colors aglow.

Limerick about Music

In the notes, we find our soul,
With the rhythm and beat, we're whole,
We're lost in the melody,
With the sounds that set us free,
Music, the healing that makes us whole.

"Wartime Toll"

Battle lines are drawn with pride,
The soldiers march, with courage aside.
Flags wave, in the wind, so high,
A symbol, of freedom, that cannot die.

The shots ring out, in the battlefield,
The brave, fall, with honor sealed.
The war drums beat, a rhythmic sound,
A call to arms, with freedom found.

The price of war, is steep, indeed,
With lives lost, and families in need.
But still, we fight, for what is right,
For freedom's cause, with all our might.

So let us honor, those who have fallen,
And the sacrifice, they have given.
For freedom, is not free, my friend,
And the price of war, until the very end.

Limerick about Art

On the canvas, we paint and we draw,
With every stroke, it's like a thaw,
We create a world so grand,
With colors and shapes that we command,
Art, the beauty that we saw.

"The Promise of Spring"

The sun rises early, and the sky is clear
The air is fresh, and the breeze is near
The promise of spring, is in the air
A season of renewal, without a care

The world is alive, with color and sound
The flowers bloom, and the bees all around
A symphony of life, that nature composes
In the promise of spring, the world discloses

So let us embrace the beauty so rare
And bask in the warmth, of the sun so fair
For spring is a time, of new beginnings
And in its promise, our spirits are winning.

Limerick about Photography

With the lens, we capture the light,
In every frame, it's a wondrous sight,
With every shot, we freeze the time,
With every click, it's like a chime,
Photography, the art that shines so bright.

"Joys of Childhood"

The joys of childhood, a time so carefree,
A world so innocent, a life so full of glee.
With laughter so loud, and dreams so bright,
And a happiness so real, that shines so bright.

For childhood is a time, of magic and wonder,
And a world so pure, that's full of blunder.
And it's a time to grow, and learn and explore,
And a time to create, memories that will endure.

So let's cherish the joys, of childhood so bright,
And let's hold on tight, to the memories that shine.
For childhood is a time, of pure happiness,
And a world so real, that's full of bliss.

Haiku: Friendship

A friend by your side,
A hand to hold in the dark,
Life's meaning in bonds.

Haiku: Family

A home full of love,
A hearth where memories thrive,
Life's meaning in roots.

"Rain From Above"

A blessing from above, a shower of grace,
The raindrops they fall, with such gentle pace.
A lullaby sung, by the winds that blow,
As the world below, is refreshed and aglow.

A cleansing of earth, a washing of air,
A gift from the heavens, beyond compare.
A symphony of sound, as the rain hits the ground,
A melody that soothes, the soul all around.

So let us embrace, this gift from above,
And be thankful for the rain, and its gentle dove.
For it brings new life, and a fresh start anew,
A blessing from above, that's forever true.

Haiku: Love

A heart full of love,
A life filled with care and grace,
The meaning found here.

Haiku: Nature

A walk in the woods,
The whispers of the breeze, life,
Nature's rhythm flows.

"The Choice is Mine"

I stand before a fork in the road
A decision to be made, a story to unfold
Do I take the path of least resistance?
Or do I brave the unknown with persistence?

The choice is mine, the power is within
To shape my destiny, to let my soul win
Do I play it safe, or do I take a leap of faith?
The answers lie within, the choice is mine to make.

So I'll take a deep breath, and close my eyes
And trust my instincts, and the stars in the skies
For life is a journey, and I am the driver
And the destination, is up to me to deliver.

Haiku: Creativity

A canvas to paint,
A page to write your story,
Life's meaning in art.

Haiku: Hope

A light in the dark,
A beacon that guides your way,
Life's meaning in hope.

"A Story in Stone"

A stonewall stands tall, rooted deep in the earth,
With a story to tell, of its humble birth.
Built brick by brick, with care and sweat,
It tells of a time, that we can't forget.

It's seen the sunrise, and the sunset,
It's felt the rain pour, and the wind blow.
It's stood the test of time, through war and peace,
A symbol of strength, and a release.

Its stones are worn, with a story to tell,
Of a life that was lived, and a love that still dwells.
So let's take a moment, to stand by its side,
And listen to its story, that it holds inside.

Haiku: Service

A life of service,
A hand to those in need, life,
Meaning in kindness.

Haiku: Faith

A prayer in the night,
A hope that guides us through life,
Meaning found in faith.

"At Sunrise"

As the world slumbers, the sky awakens,
With colors that paint the heavens.
Reds, pinks, and purples, blend so well,
A masterpiece of beauty that can only be found in a sunrise.

The birds sing a cheerful tune,
And the morning dew shines like the light of the moon.
The world feels new, and the air feels clean,
As the sun rises, and the day begins.

Oh, how beautiful it is to witness this sight,
A reminder of life's beauty, and of its might.
So let us take a moment to bask in the glow,
And let the sunrise fill us with peace, love, and hope.

Haiku: Learning

A quest to explore,
A thirst for knowledge and growth,
Meaning in learning.

Haiku: Gratitude

A heart full of thanks,
A joy in the little things,
Meaning found in thanks.

"The Consequence of Tardiness"

The clock ticks away, with a steady hand,
And I'm left behind, in a foreign land,
Where the minutes fly by, like grains of sand,
And I'm trapped in the past, with no understanding.

I remember the days, when I was on time,
With a schedule that fit, like a glove that's just right,
But now I'm lost, in a world that's unkind,
Where being late, is a constant reminder of my decline.

And so I pay the price, for my carelessness,
With the consequences that follow my distress,
For in this world, time contains preciousness,
And I must learn, to value it with my whole heart's address.

Haiku: Adventure

A path uncharted,
A journey into the unknown,
Life's meaning in thrill.

Haiku: Dreams

A vision of life,
A world of hope and desire,
Meaning in our dreams.

"Flower Dance"

The dance of the flowers, a show so divine,
A beauty so vivid, a wonder so fine.
With petals that sway, and colors so bright,
And a fragrance so sweet, that fills up the light.

For flowers are the gifts, of nature so true,
And they bring us the joy, of a world that's so new.
And they offer a feast, to the bees and the birds,
And they bring us the peace, of a love that's so heard.

So let's watch the dance, of the flowers so bright,
And let's cherish the gift, of their beauty so right.
For flowers are the treasures, of our world so fair,
And they bring us the joy, of a love that's so rare.

Haiku: Courage

A leap of faith, life,
A heart filled with boldness and might,
Courage is the key.

Haiku: Compassion

A heart full of love,
A hand to hold in the dark,
Compassion's the light.

"Never leaves my side"

The dog who never leaves my side,
A faithful friend, I cannot hide.
With a wag of the tail, and a bark so bright,
And a love that shines, both day and night.

Through rain and snow, and sun and storm,
You're always there, to keep me warm.
With a nuzzle and a kiss, and a paw on my knee,
You bring me comfort, peace, and glee.

For you are more, than just a dog,
You are a friend, who's always there, just like a rock.
And I'm so grateful, for the love that you bring,
My faithful companion, a joy to everything.

Haiku: Forgiveness

A burden released,
A heart that's free from the past,
Forgiveness brings peace.

Haiku: Purpose

A life with a goal,
A journey with a clear aim,
Meaning found in purpose.

"The Fireflies' Dance"

In the night, as the stars come out,
A magic unfolds, with a flicker and shout.
The fireflies dance, with their lights so bright,
In a symphony, of color and light.

They twirl and spin, in a graceful show,
Their wings aglow, with a soft yellow glow.
A mesmerizing sight, that's hard to miss,
A performance, of nature's pure bliss.

So let the fireflies, lead you astray,
In a dance of light, that will make your day.
And feel their magic, as they take flight,
In a show of beauty, that's truly a sight.

Haiku: Mindfulness

A life in the now,
A moment in perfect peace,
Mindfulness prevails.

Haiku: Resilience

A heart that's broken,
A life that's filled with struggle,
Resilience survives.

"Dance of Leaves"

The dance of leaves, as they fall from the trees,
A symphony of colors, as far as the eye can see.
A rustle and rustle, with each gentle breeze,
A kaleidoscope of hues, that will never cease.

The orange and the yellow, the red and the gold,
All swirling and twirling, as they're growing old.
The greens of summer, now faded and gone,
Leaving behind, a landscape so adorned.

So let us take in, this dance so serene,
And let the beauty, of fall leaves be seen.
For soon they will wither, and fall to the ground,
A reminder that change, is all around.

Haiku: Graciousness

A heart full of grace,
A life that's humble and kind,
Graciousness abounds.

Haiku: Legacy

A life well-lived, life,
A story that echoes on,
Legacy remains.

Villanelle about the Ocean

The ocean, vast and blue and deep,
It calls to us, a siren's song.
A restless wonder we long to keep.

Its waves crash hard against the steep,
A never-ending dance, so strong.
The ocean, vast and blue and deep.

The sea holds secrets that it will keep,
And stories of sailors lost and gone.
A restless wonder we long to keep.

The ocean's beauty is ours to reap,
From shore to shore it stretches long.
The ocean, vast and blue and deep.

And when we stand upon its leap,
And hear the waves, so loud and strong,
A restless wonder we long to keep.

Oh, ocean, with your timeless keep,
You are a wonder that can't be wrong.
The ocean, vast and blue and deep,
A restless wonder we long to keep.

Acrostic poem for "BEAR"

Brave in nature, with a spirit that's like a cue
Enduring in winter, with a hibernate that's like a view
Active in forage, with a taste that's like a queue
Resourceful in fishing, with a skill that's like a hue

"The Changing Tides"

The winds of change have come my way
And with it, comes a brand new day
The future looks uncertain, that's true
But I'll face it, with a heart so bright and anew

For life is full of surprises and twists
But with every bend, I'll just stand and exist
I'll face the storm, and make it through
For life's about moving forward, that I knew

So I'll embrace the changes, with a smile so wide
And I'll find my way, wherever life may guide
For every new beginning, marks an end
And with it, comes a chance to start again

Haiku: Wolf

The wolf's piercing howl,
Echoing in the dark woods,
Nature's symphony.

Haiku: Bushy tail

Squirrel, nimble and quick,
In the trees it leaps and bounds,
Nature's acrobat.

"Friendship"

The power of friendship, a bond so divine,
A connection so real, it can conquer time.
With a strength so unbreakable, and a trust so true,
And a love that endures, in the best and worst too.

For friends are the ones, who help us to grow,
And they lift us up high, when we're feeling low.
And they challenge us, to be our best self,
And they believe in us, even when no one else.

So let's honor the bond, of friendship so dear,
And let's nurture the love, and keep it so near.
For friends are the ones, who give us our might,
And they bring us the joy, of a love that shines light.

Haiku: The rabbit

The rabbit's soft fur,
A gift from nature's bounty,
Nature's comfort zone.

Haiku: Wolf eyes

The wolf's golden eyes,
A window to the wild woods,
Nature's mystery.

"Song of the Trees"

The song of the trees, a melody so grand,
A whisper of leaves, a rustle so grand.
With branches that sway, and roots so strong,
And a beauty so vast, that can never be wrong.

For trees are the lungs, of our planet so green,
And they breathe in our air, and they purify clean.
And they offer a home, to the creatures we share,
And they bring us the peace, of a life that's so rare.

So let's listen to the song, of the trees so tall,
And let's cherish the gift, of their life that stands tall.
For trees are the treasures, of our world so bright,
And they bring us the peace, of a love that shines light.

Haiku: Fallen trees

Fallen tree lies still
Memories of life and growth
Nature's final bow

Haiku: Moss on rocks

Green moss on the rocks
A soft blanket on hard stone
Nature's soothing touch

"Little Acorn"

A tiny seed, so small and round,
Lies beneath the oak tree's crown.
It starts to grow, so strong and bold,
A promise of the oak tree to hold.

It sprouts up tall, reaching high,
A source of food for creatures nigh.
A source of shelter, too, they say,
A home for squirrels, come what may.

And when it's old, and strong, and wise,
It will spread its branches to the skies.
It will stand tall, with roots so deep,
A home for all, a shelter to keep.

So next time you see an acorn small,
Remember this tale, and you'll know it all.
A symbol of growth, and life, and love,
The little acorn, sent from above.

Haiku: Song birds

The song of the bird,
Floating on the morning breeze,
Nature's sweetest gift.

"Searching Complete"

The search is over, the journey complete,
With the love that I've found, so very sweet,
And the joy that fills my heart, with each day,
And the happiness, that's here to stay.

The roads I've traveled, have led me to this place,
With the love that I've found, and the smile on my face,
And the search is over, with this love so true,
And the happiness, that I've found in you.

So I'll cherish this love, and hold it tight,
And bask in the happiness, that shines so bright,
And I'll thank the heavens, for this love so dear,
And the search is over, and the future is clear.

Puddles of rain

Puddles of rain form
Nature's temporary art
A mirror for the sky

Busy streets

The busy street roars
Hustle and bustle of the town
Nature finds a way

"Snowflake's Delicate Design"

The snowflakes fall, with a delicate touch,
In a world so pure, that's covered in white so much.
Each one unique, with a design so rare,
A creation of beauty, that's truly beyond compare.

The snow piles high, in a world so bright,
A playground of dreams, that's full of delight.
A world of wonder, in each step you take,
A breathtaking journey, that's well worth the stake.

So let the snowflakes, be your guide,
In a world of peace, where you can find pride.
And feel their beauty, as they twirl and dance,
In a show of elegance, that's truly enchanting.

Acrostic poem for "LEOPARD"

LIberating in spirit, with a soul that's like a cue
Elegant in coat, with a beauty that's like a hue
Observant in hunt, with a skill that's like a queue
Powerful in motion, with a leap that's like a hue
Active in the jungle, with a life that's like a few
Resourceful in camouflage, with a craft that's like a cue
Dashing in speed, with a sprint that's like a view

Villanelle about the Forest

The forest, green and wild and free,
It calls to us, a beckoning sound.
A place where we can simply be.

The trees, so tall, they tower to see,
Their branches spread like arms around.
The forest, green and wild and free.

A place where all the creatures can flee,
A haven where they can be unbound.
A place where we can simply be.

The leaves, so bright, like golden tea,
A carpet of colors on the ground.
The forest, green and wild and free.

A place of beauty, we can agree,
Where all the senses can be found.
A place where we can simply be.

Oh, forest, with your deep-set key,
You are a treasure that is renowned.
The forest, green and wild and free,
A place where we can simply be.

Haiku: Farmers market

At the farmers' stand
Nature's bounty is on show
Fresh food, pure and real

Ode to a Mountain

Oh, mountain, how you stand so tall,
A beacon that can never fall.
You rise up from the earth below,
A testament to nature's show.

Your peaks, so rugged, sharp, and steep,
Are like a challenge for us to keep.
You are a symbol of our might,
A call to us to rise and fight.

You hold the secrets of the land,
Of ancient times and nature's hand.
You speak to us of what we are,
Of strength and courage, near and far.

So here's to you, dear mountain grand,
A wonder of this wondrous land.

Ode to a Full Moon
Oh, full moon, how you shine so bright,
A silver disk that glows at night.
You cast a spell upon the earth,
A beacon of the world's rebirth.

Your light, so bright, so pure, so true,
A symbol of a world anew.
You guide us through the darkest hour,
And fill our hearts with inner power.

You are a wonder of the sky,
A light that guides us as we try.
So here's to you, dear full moon round,
A treasure that will always astound.

"Guardians of the Flames"

The guardians of the flames, with courage so bright,
With bravery and strength, they stand ready to fight,
Against the fire's deadly rage, day and night,
And keep us safe, with their unwavering might.

With their fire trucks and hoses, they charge into the fray,
And with their skill and training, they battle the blaze,
And in the face of danger, they never sway,
For they are the guardians of the flames, who always stand their way.

So let us take a moment, and show our gratitude,
For the sacrifices they make, and their bravery that's so true,
For they are the heroes in uniform, who always stand tall,
And their courage and bravery, will never fall.

Ode to a Seashell

Oh, seashell, from the ocean deep,
Your beauty is a joy to keep.
Your curves, your lines, your subtle shades,
Are like a work of art that fades.

You hold the memories of the sea,
Of waves that crash and winds that be.
You are a token of the past,
A symbol of a life that lasts.

You speak to us of distant lands,
Of pirate ships and far-off sands.
So here's to you, dear seashell bright,
A treasure that we hold so tight.

"Solitude"

Solitude's embrace, a familiar friend,
A comfort in the quiet, as the day comes to an end,
A time to be with oneself, to reflect and ponder,
To embrace the peace, and let the heart wander.

But sometimes, the silence, can be deafening and cold,
A reminder of the loneliness, that grows old,
And in the stillness, the mind starts to race,
And the heart aches, with the memories of a better place.

So when the loneliness creeps in, and the night grows still,
Remember that you are never truly alone, and always will,
Find comfort in the moments, and the memories that you hold,
And know that you are loved, and worth more than gold.

Ode to a Ray of Sunlight

Oh, ray of sunlight, how you shine,
Your warmth, your glow, is so divine.
You pierce the clouds and light the earth,
And fill the sky with endless mirth.

Your golden beams bring life and hope,
And help us all to learn and cope.
You fill our hearts with joy and love,
And lift our spirits high above.

You are a symbol of the light,
A shining star that guides us right.
So here's to you, dear ray of sun,
A treasure that can never be outdone.

"A Monument of Time"

A stone wall stands tall, in a field of green,
A monument of time that has always been.
Built with care, and a steady hand,
It tells the story of a simpler land.

The stones are rough, and the mortar is strong,
Built to last, for generations to come.
Its presence is felt, even from afar,
A symbol of resilience, and a shining star.

The wall has seen, the changing of the seasons,
The laughter of children, and the tears of reason.
It stands steadfast, as a reminder of our past,
A source of comfort that will forever last.

Ode to a Butterfly

Oh, butterfly, with wings so bright,
You bring a sense of pure delight.
You dance upon the summer breeze,
And flit between the flowers and trees.

Your colors, bold and brilliant hues,
Are like a rainbow come to choose.
And when you land upon a bloom,
You bring it life, you end its gloom.

You are a symbol of new life,
A creature free from strife and strife.
So here's to you, dear butterfly,
A wonder that will never die.

"The Sunset's Radiant Glow"

The ship glides on, as the sun begins to set,
In a sky of orange, that glows with no regret.
The day is ending, but the memories remain,
Of laughter and joy, that we've shared today.

The sun dips low, in a sky of gold,
A final farewell, to a day that's so bold.
The night begins, with a sky so clear,
A world of stars, which we hold so dear.

So let the sun, be your guide,
In a world of memories, where you can find pride.
And feel its warmth, as it says goodbye,
In a show of beauty, that's truly a sight.

Acrostic poem for "LION"

Loyal to pride, it's like a heart so true
Impressive in mane, with a beauty that's like a view
Opulent in presence, with a grace that's like a review
Nimble in chase, with a prowess that's like a hue

"Majestic Voyage"

The ship moves on, in a world so wide,
With endless adventure, waiting by its side.
The sea is calling, and we answer its call,
With a journey of discovery, that's truly enthralling.

The ship sails on, in a world so bright,
With endless horizons, that's full of light.
The sea whispers tales, of distant shores,
Of adventure and mystery, that's waiting to be explored.

So let the ship, be your guide,
In a world of adventure, where you can find pride.
And feel its breeze, as it takes you far,
In a journey of discovery, that's truly a star.

Acrostic poem for "KOALA"

Knocked-out in sleep, with a rest that's like a cue
Observant in eucalyptus, with a taste that's like a queue
Adorable in look, with a beauty that's like a hue
Loyal to home, with a bond that's like a glue
Active in movement, with a climb that's like a hue

Villanelle about a Snowflake

The snowflake, pure and crystal bright,
A wonder that falls from above.
A thing of beauty, so light and white.

It dances down from the winter night,
A tiny flake, a symbol of love.
The snowflake, pure and crystal bright.

It lands so soft, so out of sight,
And blankets the world with a gentle glove.
A thing of beauty, so light and white.

With every flake, a new delight,
A masterpiece, a work of art to behold.
The snowflake, pure and crystal bright.

Oh, winter wonder, so fleeting and slight,
A treasure of the season, so cold and bold.
A thing of beauty, so light and white,
The snowflake, pure and crystal bright.

Acrostic poem for "ELEPHANT"

Enormous in size, it's a gentle giant
Loyal to the herd, it's like a lion's client
Enduring in strength, with a trunk so reliant
Protective of young, it's like a loving parent
Honored in culture, it's like a legend's tyrant
Agile in movement, with grace so vibrant
Nurturing to the earth, it's like a plant reliant
Thick skin to survive, it's like a protective alliance

Villanelle about a Rose

The rose, so red, so sweet and fine,
A symbol of love and romance true.
A flower that speaks to the heart and mind.

With petals soft, like a cloud in the sky,
Its fragrance fills the air with dew.
The rose, so red, so sweet and fine.

It blossoms in the summer, so high,
And draws the bees with its honeydew.
A flower that speaks to the heart and mind.

The thorns, so sharp, a warning sign,
But beauty prevails, it's always true.
The rose, so red, so sweet and fine.

Oh, how we love this flower divine,
A gift of nature, so pure and new.
A flower that speaks to the heart and mind,
The rose, so red, so sweet and fine.

Acrostic poem for "PANTHER"

Powerful in nature, with a grace that's like a cue
Active in hunt, with a skill that's like a hue
Nimble in motion, with a leap that's like a cue
Tenacious in pursuit, with a spirit that's like a view
Handsome in coat, with a beauty that's like a hue
Energetic in play, with a heart that's like a cue
Resourceful in stealth, with a craft that's like a glue

"The Mountain's Height"

The mountain stands tall, a behemoth of might,
Its peak so high, in a breathtaking sight.
A challenge to those, who dare to climb,
With a reward of beauty, in each step in time.

The view from above, a sea of green and blue,
With a panoramic sight, that will make you feel brand new.
A world of wonder, in each step you take,
A breathtaking journey, that's well worth the stake.

So let the mountain, be your guide,
In a journey of life, where you can find pride.
And feel its power, as it towers high,
In a world of beauty, that touches the sky.

Acrostic poem for "PENGUIN"

Proud in its waddle, it's like a march so true
Elegant in tuxedo, with a coat of black and blue
Nimble in the water, with a grace that's like new
Gregarious in groups, with a song that's like a cue
Unwavering in winter, with a spirit so true
Insulated in feathers, with a coat that's like a glue
Nesting in colonies, with a life that's like a queue

"Strength of the Forest"

The strength of the trees, so tall and so grand,
A fortress of nature, and a symbol of the land.
With roots that dig deep, and reach for the sky,
And a spirit that endures, and never does die.

For the forest is life, and the life of the earth,
And it provides for us all, from its depths of rebirth.
With a bounty of fruit, and a wealth of resources,
And a balance that sustains, and never does lose us.

So let's cherish the forest, and protect its might,
And let's always remember, its importance to our sight.
For the forest is more, than just trees and the breeze,
It's the home of the wild, and the soul of the trees.

Acrostic poem for "JAGUAR"

Jumping in bounds, with a leap that's like a cue
Agile in motion, with a grace that's like a hue
Gorgeous in coat, with a beauty that's like a view
Unwavering in strength, with a power that's like a cue
Ardent in hunt, with a skill that's like a hue
Resourceful in jungle, with a life that's like a few

"Pine Cone's Beauty"

A treasure of the forest, hidden from view,
The pinecone rests a beauty so true.
Its scales, so finely crafted, form a pattern,
A work of art, nature's finest addition.

The pine cone opens, and spreads its seeds,
A gift to the earth, so nature may feed.
And when it's time, the pine cone will close,
And wait for the wind, to carry it goes.

It's a symbol of life, and growth, and change,
A reminder of the beauty, nature can arrange.
For the pinecone is more than just a cone,
It's a story of life, and the journey it's known.

Acrostic poem for "GORILLA"

Gentle in nature, with a heart so true
Opulent in strength, with a power that's like a view
Resourceful in forage, with a taste that's like a queue
Intelligent in action, with a thought that's like a cue
Loyal in group, with a bond that's like a glue
Liberating in nature, with a life that's like a few
Active in play, with a spirit that's like a hue.

"Searching"

The search for love, a journey so grand,
With twists and turns, and heartache to withstand,
And the hope that one day, I'll find the one,
And know that I'm blessed, with a love that's begun.

The roads I've traveled, have been long and rough,
With moments of doubt, and moments of love,
And the search goes on, with each step I take,
And the hope that one day, my heart will ache.

So I'll keep searching, and keep hoping, too,
That one day, I'll find the love that's true,
And my heart will sing, with a joy so bright,
And I'll know that my search, was worth the fight.

Acrostic poem for "GIRAFFE"

Gentle in nature, it's like a heart so true
Impressive in height, with a view that's like a hue
Resourceful in leaves, with a taste that's like a cue
Adept in the wild, with a grace that's like a review
Flexible in neck, with a stretch that's like a preview
Friendly in groups, with a bond that's like a glue
Enduring in the savannah, with a life that's like a few

Villanelle about a Mountain Stream

The mountain stream, with water so clear,
A wonder that flows from high above.
A thing of beauty, so crisp and dear.

It meanders through the rocks and tiers,
And babbles on, with joy and love.
The mountain stream, with water so clear.

Its currents, so swift, are never austere,
And fill the air, with a soothing lull.
A thing of beauty, so crisp and dear.

The trees, so green, they surround the sphere,
And dip their leaves, with a gentle shove.
The mountain stream, with water so clear.

Oh, how we love this water seer,
A gift of nature, like a dove.
A thing of beauty, so crisp and dear,
The mountain stream, with water so clear.

Acrostic poem for "WHALE"

Wild in the ocean, with a world that's like a view
Huge in size, with a presence that's like a hue
Active in travel, with a journey that's like a cue
Leisurely in swim, with a motion that's like a hue
Endangered in number, with a status that's like a cue

Villanelle about a Thunderstorm

The thunderstorm, with lightning so bright,
A wonder that rumbles from above.
A thing of beauty, so bold and white.

The lightning strikes, like a sword in fight,
And fills the sky, with a crackling glove.
The thunderstorm, with lightning so bright.

The thunder roars, like a voice in height,
And shakes the earth, with a mighty love.
A thing of beauty, so bold and white.

With rain, it pours, like a storm in sight,
And floods the land, with a wetting of dove.
The thunderstorm, with lightning so bright.

Oh, how we watch it, with fear and might,
A gift of nature, like a love.
A thing of beauty, so bold and white,
The thunderstorm, with lightning so bright.

Acrostic poem for "TIGER"

The king of the jungle, it's like a royal sire
Impressive in size, with a coat that's like fire
Gentle to cubs, but fierce when it requires
Elegant in motion, with a stealth that inspires
Roaming in the wild, it's like a nature's flyer

Villanelle about a Night Sky

The night sky, with stars so bright,
A wonder that twinkles up above.
A thing of beauty, so dark and light.

The stars, so many, a carpet of light,
They shine so bright, with hope and love.
The night sky, with stars so bright.

It fills our hearts, with a peaceful sight,
And stirs our souls, with a magical glove.
A thing of beauty, so dark and light.

The moon, so bright, it fills the night,
And casts its glow, with a quiet shove.
The night sky, with stars so bright.

Oh, how we marvel at this sight,
A gift of nature, like a dove.
A thing of beauty, so dark and light,
The night sky, with stars so bright.

Ode to a Pebble

Oh, pebble on the forest floor,
So small and simple, yet much more.
You hold the secrets of the earth,
Of ages past, of death and birth.

Your rough exterior, weathered by time,
Tells a story, a tale sublime.
Of rivers raging, mountains high,
And ancient oceans stretching nigh.

Your smoothness, like a river's stone,
Is evidence of beauty grown.
Of time and nature, hand in hand,
Creating something truly grand.

So here's to you, dear pebble small,
A testament to nature's thrall.
Your quiet grace and humble mien,
Remind us all of what has been.

Acrostic poem for "ZEBRA"

Zealous in stride, it's like a spirit so true
Elegant in stripes, with a beauty that's like a hue
Bold in the wild, with a grace that's like a preview
Resourceful in grasslands, with a taste that's like a queue
Active in groups, with a bond that's like a glue

"Just About Dogs"

Furry friends, four-legged grace,
Loyal companions, with a loving face.
Wagging tails, and playful barks,
Bringing joy into our lives with their sweet spark.

Their wet noses, and floppy ears,
A comforting touch, to chase away our fears.
With eyes that speak, of unconditional love,
Our dogs, sent from heaven above.

They run and play, with boundless energy,
And snuggle close, in moments of serenity.
Dogs are more than just pets, they're family,
With a bond that lasts, eternally.

From fetching sticks, to learning tricks,
Their unwavering devotion never misses a beat.
With wagging tails, and playful grins,
Our dogs, always there, to make us grin.

So here's to man's best friend, our canine muse,
Bringing us joy and never letting us lose.
A faithful companion, till the very end,
Our dogs, our love, will never bend.

Printed in Dunstable, United Kingdom

68061930R00077